THE WORLD
AROUND US

ON THE NEWS

Our First Talk About Tragedy

Dr. Jillian Roberts   Illustrations by Jane Heinrichs

ORCA BOOK PUBLISHERS

*This book is for my stepfather, Val, who as a firefighter dedicated his life
to the service of his community as a first responder.*
—JR

For Mark, who is my anchor in both calm and stormy seas.
—JH

MIX
Paper from
responsible sources
FSC® C016245
www.fsc.org

Text copyright © 2018 Jillian Roberts
Illustrations copyright © 2018 Jane Heinrichs

Library and Archives Canada Cataloguing in Publication

Roberts, Jillian, 1971–, author
On the news: our first talk about tragedy / Dr. Jillian Roberts;
illustrated by Jane Heinrichs.
(The world around us)

Issued in print and electronic formats.
ISBN 978-1-4598-1784-5 (hardcover).—ISBN 978-1-4598-1785-2 (pdf).—
ISBN 978-1-4598-1786-9 (epub)

1. Disasters—Juvenile literature. 2. Disasters—Psychological aspects—
Juvenile literature. I. Heinrichs, Jane, 1982–, illustrator II. Title.
HV553.R633 2018   j303.48'5   C2017-907930-1
C2017-907931-X

Summary: Using illustrations, full-color photographs
and straightforward text, this nonfiction picture book introduces
the topics of tragedy and disaster to young readers.

First published in the United States, 2018
Library of Congress Control Number: 2018933705

*Orca Book Publishers is dedicated to preserving the environment and has
printed this book on Forest Stewardship Council® certified paper.*

Orca Book Publishers gratefully acknowledges the support for
its publishing programs provided by the following agencies:
the Government of Canada through the Canada Book Fund and
the Canada Council for the Arts, and the Province of British Columbia
through the BC Arts Council and the Book Publishing Tax Credit.

Cover and interior art by Jane Heinrichs
Artwork created using English watercolors and
Japanese brush pens on Italian watercolor paper
Edited by Liz Kemp
Design by Rachel Page

Front cover photos: iStock.com, Shutterstock.com, iStock.com
Back cover photos: Shutterstock.com

ORCA BOOK PUBLISHERS
orcabook.com

Printed and bound in Canada.

21 20 19 18 • 4 3 2 1

When you observe the world around us,

maybe by watching or listening to the news,
you may see or hear about things that are scary and
confusing. Many good things happen in our world, but
sometimes bad things happen too. It is okay to
ask questions when you do not understand why
something bad has happened in the world.

I saw on the news today that something bad had happened in the city. Many people were hurt, and some were killed. I felt so sad and scared.

I understand how you feel. I feel the same way when I see or hear things like that on the news. The world can be a complicated and confusing place. It is hard to accept that sometimes very bad things happen in the world around us.

An ambulance responds to an emergency call in Manhattan, New York.
CLARI MASSIMILIANO/SHUTTERSTOCK.COM

What do you call something bad that happens?

The aftermath in Amatrice, Italy, following a magnitude 6.2 earthquake in 2016.
ISTOCK.COM/BEEANDBEE

When something bad happens, we often call it a "tragedy" or a "disaster."

Tragedy and Disaster have similar meanings. Both are used to describe something bad that happens. *Disaster* is most often used to describe a major event itself—an earthquake, tsunami or flood, for example. *Tragedy* is usually used when we talk about the people involved in the event.

For example, Hurricane Katrina was one of the most destructive natural disasters in US history. More than 1,200 people lost their lives in this tragedy.

"Every year, close to 160 million people are affected by natural disaster worldwide."*

—World Health Organization (WHO)

*That's almost half the population of the United States and four times the population of Canada.

What causes a tragedy or disaster?

Sometimes they are acts of nature, which means they are caused by changes in the natural world around us. Sometimes they are caused by people.

Emergency crews work to secure a building in Kyiv, Ukraine, that was damaged in an explosion caused by a gas leak, 2017.
REVIEW NEWS/SHUTTERSTOCK.COM

Children row a makeshift boat through a flooded street in Dhaka, Bangladesh, 2017.
SK HASAN ALI/SHUTTERSTOCK.COM

What kinds of tragedies are caused by nature?

Tragedies caused by nature are often called *natural disasters*. They include such events as forest fires, hurricanes, earthquakes, landslides, floods, droughts and tsunamis.

A young woman walks by wreckage from the Port-au-Prince earthquake in Haiti in 2010.
ISTOCK.COM/1001NIGHTS

A Little Bit More About Natural Disasters

The World Health Organization states that natural disasters have an immediate impact on people's lives and often cause the destruction of people's homes and communities. These disasters may affect people's health, their jobs, their families and how they live their lives for a very long time.

The 21st century has seen major natural disasters such as these:

- An earthquake in Port-au-Prince, Haiti, in 2010 affected more than three million people.
- The Boxing Day tsunami in 2004, caused by an earthquake in the Indian Ocean with a moment magnitude of 9.1 to 9.3, completely washed out parts of Sumatra.
- Hurricane Katrina struck the Gulf Coast of the United States in 2005 and is considered the most destructive hurricane of the 21st century.

What kinds of tragedies are caused by people?

Fire crews work to put out a forest fire in Portugal.
STEVE PHOTOGRAPHY/SHUTTERSTOCK.COM

Italian firefighters fly a Canadair CL-215 over a forest fire in Perugia, Italy, 2017.
SERPEBLU/SHUTTERSTOCK.COM

People cause many different kinds of tragedies. For example, they may cause fires by accidentally or intentionally setting grass, brush, trees or even buildings on fire.

Workers in hazmat suits clean up a crude-oil spill in Prao Bay, Thailand, 2013.
JUKURAE/SHUTTERSTOCK.COM

Sometimes people cause tragedies with their cars, or with boats, trains or tractors. They may do this by accident or by being irresponsible.

Firefighters work to help drivers involved in a car accident in Roseburg, Oregon.
TFOXFOTO/SHUTTERSTOCK.COM

Technological Disasters

happen when systems break down or the people controlling them make mistakes. These types of disasters include nuclear-reactor meltdowns, oil tanker and pipeline spills and train derailments.

The 20th and 21st centuries have seen technological disasters such as these:

- In 2013, an unattended freight train carrying crude oil rolled into downtown Lac-Mégantic, Quebec, and derailed. The train cars caught fire and exploded, destroying 30 buildings and killing 47 people.

- The BP oil spill in the Gulf of Mexico in 2010 was the largest marine oil spill in history. An estimated 205 million gallons of oil spilled into the gulf over 87 days. Over 30,000 people came together to collect oil, clean up beaches and take care of animals.

- The Chernobyl disaster in 1986, in what is now the Ukraine, was the most catastrophic nuclear power plant incident in history. The economic, environmental, cultural and health impacts of this disaster are still being felt today.

Police officers patrol the Trocadero gardens near the Eiffel Tower in Paris, France.
BLACKMAC/SHUTTERSTOCK.COM

Stores were ransacked during riots in Seine-Saint-Denis, France, in 2017.
JACKY D/SHUTTERSTOCK.COM

And sometimes people cause tragedies on purpose, such as when people commit crimes. Sometimes you hear about terrorism or terrorists on the news.

Terrorism is the calculated use of violence against innocent people in order to make them afraid. *Terrorists*, the people who commit crimes of terrorism, often target people who have different cultural, religious or political views.

Here are some of the major terrorist attacks that have occurred in the world:

- On September 11, 2001, nineteen men hijacked four American commercial airplanes and intentionally crashed them into buildings. There were 2,977 people killed in New York City, Washington, DC, and outside Shanksville, Pennsylvania.

- On November 13, 2015, attacks across Paris killed 130 people and wounded hundreds of others.

- On January 29, 2017, a terrorist attacked a mosque in Quebec City, killing six worshippers and injuring many others.

- On August 12, 2017, a terrorist drove his car into a crowd in Charlottesville, Virginia, killing one person and injuring 19 others.

Why do tragedies happen?

Durbar Square, a UNESCO World Heritage site, was severely damaged after an earthquake in Kathmandu, Nepal, in 2015.

Flooding in the 2011 monsoon season in Bangkok, Thailand, was severe.
PRAISAENG/SHUTTERSTOCK.COM

No one knows for sure why tragedies occur. Part of understanding tragedies is accepting that most of the time we cannot control them.

Did You Know?

Sometimes people are really mixed up. They don't understand the difference between right and wrong. It's wrong to hurt other people on purpose. When something bad happens, we should always look for ways to help those who are hurt.

A child helps collect clean water after the earthquake in Kathmandu, Nepal, in 2015.
THINK4PHOTOP/SHUTTERSTOCK.COM

What is it like for someone who experiences a tragedy?

Temporary shelters for victims of the 2015 earthquake in Kathmandu, Nepal.
DUTOURDUMONDE PHOTOGRAPHY/SHUTTERSTOCK.COM

It is very, very difficult for people who are affected by a tragedy or disaster. People in these situations experience a lot of different emotions. They can feel sad, scared and angry. As a child psychologist, I help children by talking with them about these feelings. And I want you to know it is normal to have strong emotions when a tragedy or disaster happens, even if you are just hearing about it on TV or the radio. It is also normal to worry about yourself and your family. Everyone is different, and we all react differently to tragedies and disasters.

Noula! In Haitian this means "We are here. We survive." This saying was used frequently after Hurricane Matthew in 2016.

"Bad things do happen in the world, like war, natural disasters, disease. But out of those situations always arise stories of ordinary people doing extraordinary things."

—Daryn Kagan, former broadcast journalist

Children walk beside a building that collapsed after a 2015 earthquake in the Kavrepalanchok District of Nepal.
SOMJIN KIONG-UGKARA/SHUTTERSTOCK.COM

I have my own ideas about why bad things happen from time to time. Perhaps tragedies happen to give people a chance to be strong.

Perhaps tragedies happen to give people a chance to be brave.

Rescue teams search a building that was destroyed in an earthquake in Van, Turkey, 2011.
DEEPSPACE/SHUTTERSTOCK.COM

Children watch as rescue workers comb through a building destroyed in the earthquake in Kathmandu, Nepal, in 2015.
MICHAEL YL TAN/SHUTTERSTOCK.COM

Perhaps tragedies happen to bring people together.

Tragedies and times of sadness and grief can be turned into opportunities to teach compassion.

Perhaps tragedies happen to give people a chance to be kind and caring.

When An Entire Town Came Together to Choose Kindness

During the tragedy of September 11, 2001, the United States closed its airspace, causing about 200 flights in the air to be diverted to other airports. Gander, a tiny town in Newfoundland, Canada, opened its runways, allowing 38 transatlantic flights to land. The people of Gander and surrounding fishing villages filled their schools, community rooms, homes and churches with cots for stranded passengers. They even found a way to care for 17 dogs and cats and two great apes that were aboard the planes. The people of Gander, a town of no more than 10,000, looked at all those planes lined up at the airport and didn't think about terrorism or potential attacks. They just wanted to help.

—Taken from Petula Dvorak's article in the *Washington Post*, September 10, 2016

"Whenever something negative happens, there is a deep lesson concealed in it."

—Eckhart Tolle

What is Resilience?

It is the ability to recover from or adjust to misfortune or change.

"The most beautiful people we have known are those who have known defeat, known suffering, known struggle, known loss, and have found their way out of the depths. These persons have an appreciation, a sensitivity, and an understanding of life that fills them with compassion, gentleness, and a deep loving concern. Beautiful people do not just happen."

—Elisabeth Kübler-Ross, psychiatrist

Volunteers help feed earthquake victims living in temporary shelters in Van, Turkey, 2011.
THOMAS KOCH/SHUTTERSTOCK.COM

It is terrible when a tragedy happens. However, it is important to know that life continues after a tragedy. People are resilient.

When people come together during a tragedy, and when people are strong, brave, kind and compassionate, it is easier for them to continue on with everyday life.

Children walk flooded streets in Bangkok, Thailand, in 2011.
WUTTHICHAI/SHUTTERSTOCK.COM

Volunteers make sandbags to try to protect Bangkok, Thailand, against flooding in 2011.

What can we do to help when tragedies or disasters occur in the world around us?

There are many things we can do. For example, we can show our appreciation to the first responders in our community—firefighters, police officers and paramedics. We can also show our respect to members of our community who help during these challenging times, such as doctors, nurses and other health-care workers.

And we can participate in fundraising efforts for aid organizations that do tremendous good for our global community during times of tragedy and disaster—such as Red Cross, UNICEF and Médecins Sans Frontières/Doctors Without Borders. Perhaps when you grow up, you will become a great helper in your community too!

Workers assist people during flooding in Bangkok, Thailand, in 2011.
STOCKPHOTO MANIA/SHUTTERSTOCK.COM

A Note from Dr. Jillian Roberts, Author and Child Psychologist

As a child psychologist I have spent countless hours helping children and families who have experienced tragedies. It is challenging, even as a seasoned therapist, to know what is best to say to little ones in emotional anguish. I have found the following quote by Fred Rogers (better known as Mr. Rogers) particularly helpful and inspiring to my work in these times:

> When I was a boy and I would see scary things in the news, my mother would say to me, "Look for the helpers. You will always find people who are helping." To this day, especially in times of disaster, I remember my mother's words, and I am always comforted by realizing that there are still so many helpers—so many caring people in this world.

When we look for the helpers, we can see that there is hope in times of great darkness. Helpers shine a kind of light that helps us find our way. We can then see beauty in the totality of the human experience. I hope this book inspires each reader to be a helper, in any way possible, in times of tragedy and disaster. When we come together and show strength, courage, kindness and compassion, we help make the world around us a much better place.

Resources

Books for Children

Holmes, Margaret M. *A Terrible Thing Happened.*
  Washington, DC: Magination Press, 1993.

Ippen, Chandra Ghosh. *Once I Was Very Very Scared.*
  San Francisco, CA: Piplo Productions, 2017.

Roberts, Jillian. *What Happens When a Loved One Dies?*
  Victoria, BC: Orca Book Publishers, 2016.

Books for Parents

Levine, Peter A. and Maggie Kline. *Trauma Through a Child's Eyes:
  Awakening the Ordinary Miracle of Healing.* Berkeley, CA: North
  Atlantic Books, 2006.

Monahon, Cynthia. *Children and Trauma: A Guide for Parents and
  Professionals.* San Francisco, CA: Jossey-Bass, 1997.

van der Kolk, Bessel. *The Body Keeps the Score: Brain, Mind, and Body
  in the Healing of Trauma.* New York, NY: Viking Press, 2014.

*I would like to extend my gratitude to my expert readers,
Dr. Natalee Popadiuk and Dr. Tim Black, who took the time to
carefully review the words in this book and share their insights.*
—Dr. Jillian Roberts

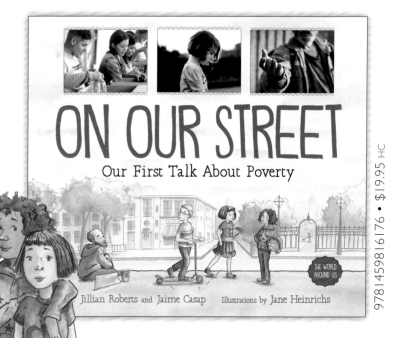

ON OUR STREET

Our First Talk About Poverty

Jillian Roberts and Jaime Casap   Illustrations by Jane Heinrichs

978 1 4598 1 6176 • $19.95 HC

Child psychologist Dr. Jillian Roberts covers topics such as:

- poverty and homelessness
- tragedy and disaster
- prejudice and bullying
- Internet safety
- body health and consent
- environmental stewardship

AGES 6–8 • 32 PAGES
FULL-COLOR PHOTOGRAPHS • RESOURCES INCLUDED

These **inquiry-based books** are an excellent **cross-curricular resource** encouraging children to explore and discuss important issues and foster their own **compassion and empathy**. Sidebars offer further reading for older children or care providers who have bigger questions. For younger children just starting to make these observations, the simple **question-and-answer** format of the main text will provide a foundation of knowledge on the subject matter.

TheWorldAroundUsSeries.com